Treasures of the Heart

D1425009

'Modern Spirituality' series

Treasures of the Heart

DAILY READINGS WITH
JEAN VANIER

Edited by Sister Benedict Gaughan OSB

with an introduction by
Sheila Cassidy

DARTON·LONGMAN + TODD

First published in 1989 by
Darton, Longman and Todd Ltd
1 Spencer Court
140–142 Wandsworth High Street
London SW18 4JJ

Reprinted 1991, 1994 and 1996

© 1989 Jean Vanier
Arrangement © 1989 Sister Benedict Gaughan OSB
Introduction © 1989 Sheila Cassidy

British Library Cataloguing in Publication Data

Vanier, Jean
    Treasures of the heart.
    1. Christian life – Devotional works
    I. Title   II. Gaughan, Benedict   III. Series
    242

    ISBN 0–232–51821–1

Phototypeset by Intype, London
Printed and bound in Great Britain by
Page Bros, Norwich

Contents

Introduction

Jean Vanier is regarded by many as one of the
spiritual giants of our time, a man marked out by
personal holiness and by the amazing flowering of
his work of caring for the handicapped in the
movements of l'Arche and Faith and Light. After
three years, I still find myself surprised by joy at
knowing Jean no longer as a hero but as a friend,
a man with whom I can weep or laugh, talk or
pray or simply share whatever is in my heart – or
indeed whatever is left over in the kitchen when I
find suddenly that I am starving!

So that you may better understand and appreci-
ate Jean's words and ideas I've been asked to write
a little about the man who wrote them.

The first thing to say about Jean Vanier is that
he is a BIG man: he is tall of stature, well educated,
broad of vision and deeply wise, with a truly enor-
mous heart.

Jean is a French-Canadian, born in Geneva in
1928, the son of General George Vanier who,
later, became Governor General of Canada. He
has three brothers, one of whom is a Cistercian
monk, and one sister, Thérèse, who is a doctor.
Jean's was a wartime childhood, and in 1942,
aged thirteen, he told his father that he wanted to
go to England to join the Navy. Just what General
Vanier made of his son's ambitions we do not
know but, incredibly, he said 'I trust you' and
gave Jean permission to go. In order to understand
the absurdity of this schoolboy ambition we must
remember that not only was Jean merely thirteen

but that England was at war and one in every three troopships was being torpedoed as it crossed the Atlantic. Jean sees his father's acceptance of his request as one of the most important moments of his life: for, he says, 'if a much loved and respected father will trust you to do something apparently so foolhardy, then you can trust yourself'. History does not relate what Pauline Vanier thought of the whole idea but in 1942 Jean travelled alone on a troopship to Liverpool and made his way, equally alone, to London and then to Dartmouth Naval College in Devon where he was enrolled as a Cadet.

It was in this naval milieu, then, that Jean spent his adolescence and early manhood and it was there too that he became slowly drawn towards the idea of life consecrated to God. His was not a Damascus road experience but more a gradual movement towards things of the spirit. He finds it hard to say when it began – there were a number of factors: his brother Benedict's entry into a Cistercian monastery, friendship with a Carmelite nun, and then the reading of Thomas Merton's *The Seven-Storey Mountain*. I laughed so much when he told me this for I too had been deeply influenced by the same book, 12,000 miles away, as a schoolgirl in an Australian convent. Thomas Merton, the wild young writer and poet who entered a Trappist monastery in the Kentucky hills and then wrote so vividly about his thirst for God, must have touched so many hearts in the 1940s and early 1950s.

So, Jean listened to these stirrings in his heart and began to go to daily Mass, setting out at six in the morning on his bicycle and returning, sometimes, to the taunts of his fellow officers. In hindsight, he says that he knew, even then, that he was being led away from the Navy – that it was just a question of time.

In 1948, Jean rediscovered his Canadian roots and transferred to the Royal Canadian Navy. His sense of religious vocation, however, crossed the Atlantic with him, and in 1950, feeling the time had come, he resigned his commission and embarked upon the search for his own particular way to God. He was, at this time, twenty-one years old.

I find myself endlessly fascinated by the phenomenon of religious call, because it seems to me to be one of the clearest ways we have of seeing the mysterious manner in which God works. Why should a young man, destined for a promising naval career, abandon it all in search of a way to follow the Gospel more closely – I don't know and I suspect Jean didn't either. He simply knew himself called by name, into the unknown, like Moses, Abraham, Peter, Paul and so many others.

When I asked him where he went from there, he grinned and said, 'I wrote three letters, two to Jesuits and one to a Dominican, Père Thomas Philippe, an old friend of the family.' Those Jesuits, it seems, had little time for the earnest searchings of a God-struck twenty-one-year-old, but Père Thomas, then chaplain to a student community in Paris, wrote with such warmth and enthusiasm that Jean had no hesitation in accepting his invitation to join him and set out once again for Europe.

Eau Vive was an exciting place to be, a community of some eighty students studying at le Saulchoir, the Dominican Faculty of Theology and Philosophy. These were formative years and Jean was greatly influenced by the leader of the community, Père Thomas Philippe, sensing perhaps even then that their ways to God were inextricably linked. In 1952, Père Thomas left the community on health grounds and Jean took over its leadership. There followed a period of some difficulty as the Dominicans were not happy to see a layman as director of the community and suspended the students' right to study at le Saulchoir. Many students left but a faithful remnant remained, making the hour's journey each day into Paris to study at the university.

During the year that followed, Jean was accepted as a candidate to the priesthood for the diocese of Quebec but he continued as director of the community whilst pursuing his studies in Paris. In 1956, however, there was another period of crisis and confusion in the community and Jean was once more thrown into uncertainty as to his calling. This time, however, things were more serious and not only did he resign from his position as leader of the community but decided to abandon his studies for the priesthood. He entered upon another period of intense searching and reflection. The first year was spent living in the guesthouse at the Trappist monastery of Belle Fontaine. Then followed a further year of solitude on a farm, while he worked on his doctorate, near Aigle. In 1959 he built a house in the little village of Fatima, and this remained his base for the next few years until he obtained his doctorate in Philosophy at the Institut Catholique in Paris.

In 1964 Jean became a visiting Professor at St Michael's College in the University of Toronto, giving a course on justice issues. He comments wryly that the rather modest attendance at his lectures swelled dramatically when he changed his subject matter to issues of love, friendship and sexuality! All seemed set for an academic career, but once again his direction changed.

In order to understand the next stage in the journey one must focus attention not on Toronto but upon a quiet French village, hidden in the forest surrounding the town of Compiègne, about ninety kilometres north of Paris. It was here, in the village of Trosly Breuil, that Jean's teacher and mentor Père Thomas Philippe also began a new life – as chaplain to a home of handicapped adult men. The home – an elegant château known as the Val Fleuri – had been started by a Monsieur Prat for his son, Jean Pierre, who was mentally handicapped. Working in collaboration with a well-known psychiatrist, Dr Préaut, in whose house Jean had been a lodger, they soon welcomed other needy men until 'the Val' was home to some thirty handicapped men. In 1963 Jean came to visit Père Thomas at Trosly and they discussed the possibility that it was here, among the most vulnerable of mind and spirit, that Jean might find an end to his search for a truly Christian community.

Incredibly, it seemed to Jean that he had come home and, with the decisiveness that so often characterizes an answer to call, he left his academic career in Toronto, bought a dilapidated house in Trosly and 'welcomed' his two first companions, Raphael and Philippe, both men from an institute for the mentally handicapped.

Jean called his little community l'Arche (the Ark), that unwieldy boat in which Noah sheltered such a motley collection of God's creatures. The first Ark was true to its name. There was Louis, the Canadian architect, Henri, the Frenchman, Raphael and Philippe and of course Jean, who must have seemed like the giraffe, towering over his fellow shipmates. How in God's name did he expect it all to work? Jean had no experience of mentally handicapped people, no training in running a therapeutic community. By all expectations, the whole foolish venture should have failed. But it didn't – to everyone's surprise, it flourished. Why? The answer, I suspect, lies in the fact of Jean's amazing gift of openness and humility. I can do no better than quote his own words:

'But it was from Raphael and Philippe that I really began to learn. I suppose in receiving them from an asylum I felt good, a sort of "saviour". I had, so I thought, the right to tell them what to do. They were in some way under my power and they should fit into my project. Without any doubt, in starting l'Arche, I wanted to create a Christian community. I had to discover little by little, however, that this was not Raphael's and Philippe's major concern. They needed friendship and security, someone who really cared for them and who listened to their needs and desires and to what they had to say. I had to learn that l'Arche was not just my project but also Raphael's and Philippe's and that of many others who were to come to l'Arche and put their roots down there. I had to discover something about welcome and respect for people, something about liberation of hearts and patience. I had much to learn about myself and my faults and defects, my need to dominate and command after spending eight years in the Navy. I had to learn about human growth and suffering, about sharing, and about the ways of God.'

In March of the following year, 1965, the director of the Val Fleuri and most of his staff resigned and Jean was asked to replace him. He writes: 'I was thus plunged into the chaotic world of thirty handicapped men. There was much depression and violence there and I felt terribly inadequate. Little by little, people came to help: never many, just enough. Meals gradually became times of celebration. We started to pray together in the house and we went on a pilgrimage to Lourdes. Peace began to enter into the hearts of people. Work in the workshops became serious and important seeds of hope started to spring up. L'Arche was becoming a family for those who did not have one and a place of growth for all.'

There is no space here to tell the story of the growth and flowering of l'Arche. From those seeds of love, openness and respect there has emerged an amazing movement: a network of communities of love and hospitality in which helpers and handicapped people live together, sharing their lives, their frustrations, their hopes and their tears. It remains a gospel-based movement, gathering to itself a motley of people mostly, but not exclusively, Christians. As in the early days the Ark is home to a great variety of people: wounded men and women of all creeds and none, people vowed in celibacy, young people searching and married couples. Some people stay for a year or two, some for many years, a few for life and a great many for just a few days or weeks. There are l'Arche communities all over the world now, in Africa, Asia, South America and Europe. Trosly Breuil remains the largest, with around 200 handicapped and as many helpers living in houses scattered throughout Trosly and nearby villages.

And Jean: what of the man who began it all, some twenty-five years ago? Has he, like Francis, been crushed by the child of his dreams or has he grown into a fat-cat guru, cherished and emasculated on a flower-bedecked throne? Not at all! Jean Vanier still lives at l'Arche, in one room, not far from his original house. He still eats his meals at the Val Fleuri and he still talks and laughs and prays with the wounded and the strong. In 1980 he stepped down from the leadership of the community and now spends much of his time on the road, visiting the various communities of l'Arche or Faith and Light throughout the world, listening, encouraging, and planning for future development.

His gifts of communication which drew the Toronto students to his talks on interpersonal relationships have flowered over the years and he is a powerful speaker, retreat-giver and broadcaster. His message is always devastatingly simple: about the love of Jesus, his presence in the poor and in our own fragility and the need for love and acceptance in a broken world.

What impresses me about Jean is his wisdom, his gentle manner and his listening. He spends hours and hours of every day listening to the searching youngsters, weary assistants, the angry, the anguished and the joyful. It is from this knowledge of people, inextricably interwoven with his knowledge of God and of himself that his ideas are distilled. It is important not to be misled by the simplicity of his language – indeed he has a way of using words that is peculiarly his own. He speaks often of the 'littleness' of people, of their woundedness, their fragility, their brokenness, when perhaps others would speak more of emotional distress or neurosis. I believe that Jean's is a language worth learning because it is a language of hope, the vehicle for a message which tells us to stop pretending to be good or clever or whole and admit that we are frail and flawed because that's the way everyone is: that's the way God made people, and that's the way he loves them.

SHEILA CASSIDY

The secret things of God

Jesus tells us of his love for his Father. He is in love with the Father. When he tells us that we must become like little children, he means that we must become like him before his Father. Jesus is incredibly little. How quickly we want to prove ourselves and show how we are better than others. All Jesus wants to do is to be in communion with the Father whom he loves. He becomes transparent. The Father flows through him so that when we see Jesus we see the Father. They are so united. Jesus wants us to see him in one another; he reveals the Father and we reveal Jesus one to another . . .

There is an intimate link between the contemplative spirit and pain. We have a special mission. Our lives are not an escape from pain. It is not for us to run away from the pain of the world but somehow to hold onto it. It is important to hold in our prayer those who are stretched beyond their limits.

We can only do that if we become like Jesus and if we love the Father. Let Jesus love and live inside us. 'The secret things of God are hidden.'

The great secret is that in this world of pain and division, he comes and wants to reveal himself to us. He wants to say to us, 'I wish to rest in you'. This is a beautiful secret.

Jesus

He came as a tiny child in the womb of a woman. He was clothed in the vulnerability of a child in need of its mother, crying out for protection and help.

The love of a mother is the only real security an infant has; without it the life of the child is in danger of being overwhelmed by a terrible fear, a fear of death, which will block development of the emotions, the mind and the spirit.

The Almighty became a helpless child utterly dependent on a relationship with a woman, a relationship of love.

At birth Jesus had no security but the arms of Mary and the presence of Joseph. He became a child refugee as the family fled into Egypt, encountering dangers and uncertainties. And after their return they settled in the village of Nazareth . . . And there Jesus lived in simplicity for thirty years. He worked with his hands, being a son of the carpenter, Joseph . . . The word made flesh lived the humble, lowly life of a poor family. He lived the Beatitudes before announcing them.

Magnificat

All of us are called forth, with this tiny seed of the Spirit, to grow and to nourish and to heal. This is our responsibility; to go forth to all. The fruit is not for us, for our joy and plenitude, but for the people of God. We must gradually discover this power which has been given to us and is not ours; it is the Spirit and it is Jesus living in us.

It is not we who are called to do good, but the Spirit of God in us. He comes to live in us as in a temple and flows out from us to awaken the Spirit in the hearts of others, so that they too may become conscious of the beauty of their temple, so that they may discover under all the bitterness and despair the presence of God living in them and waiting to be awakened. It is a responsibility to welcome the Spirit of Jesus into our being, just as Mary carried responsibility when she welcomed his physical presence into her womb.

The first thing to do as we become conscious that we are the temple of the Spirit is to give thanks, as Mary did when she sang the Magnificat:

My soul magnifies the Lord. (Luke 1:46–49)

Have patience

We are not the masters of our own feelings of attraction or revulsion, which come from the places in ourselves over which we have little or no control. All we can do is try not to follow inclinations which make for barriers within the community. We have to hope that the Holy Spirit will come to forgive, purify and trim the rather twisted branches of our being.

Our emotional make-up has grown from a thousand fears and egoisms since our infancy, as well as from signs of love and the gift of God. It is a mixture of shadow and light. And so it will not be straightened out in a day; this will take a thousand purifications and pardons, daily efforts and above all a gift of the Holy Spirit which renews us from within.

It is a long haul to transform our emotional make-up so that we can start really loving our enemy. We have to be patient with our feelings and fears; we have to be merciful to ourselves. If we are to make the passage to acceptance and love of the other – all the others – we must start very simply, by recognizing our own blocks, jealousies, ways of comparing ourselves to others, prejudices and hatreds. We have to recognize that we are poor creatures, that we are what we are. And we have to ask our Father to forgive.

The light within

There are times when we sense the light within us, urging us forth to delight in truth, the truth in our own being, the truth of the word of God, of reality, of people. The light urges us to separate ourselves from anything which is not true, from all that is darkness, lies or illusion, for we sense that it is the truth which will set us free.

We begin to love the universe, this extraordinary universe with the stars and the moon and the sun, the winds, the seasons, the lands, the animals and the people.

We begin to look at the music and the suffering of the world. We begin to discover the beauty of the word of God and we love it. And thus gradually lose our heaviness and we begin to grow in hope. The wings of our being come forth. We begin to urge and to yearn. We are reborn in hope.

This is the light which grows in us, which urges us on to greater understanding of the beauties of people and of the universe and gradually calls us forth to wonderment and contemplation. We begin to look at this universe and at Jesus with the eyes of a child, with the peace, the excitement, the adoration of a child. This is the light as it grows in us: to love reality . . .

Living together

Jesus heals people and then calls them forth together. He calls forth Peter, John, Mary of Magdala, Paul. And he asks those he has healed and called forth to join together, live together, be together.

He desires that those he has called forth, and in whom he has put his Spirit, be united as the Father and the Son are united. He desires that their love for one another be something so special that people will know by it that they are his disciples.

Jesus calls his friends to community, where they live and share together. They are called in their unity and love for one another to be a sign of and a witness to something very special – the life of the Spirit, a rebirth, the good news.

> It is by your love for
> one another that everyone
> will recognize you
> to be my disciples. (John 13:35)

We know that we need brothers and sisters if we are to grow in the Spirit. They help us by the way they live; they encourage and strengthen us. We also know that it is easier more often to pray when we are together than when we are alone. Community is one of the most beautiful realities – brothers and sisters loving and being together. It is also one of the most difficult to accomplish.

Belonging

The sense of belonging takes time to be born. We have to go through passages that are more or less painful before it comes to birth or reaches fulfilment.

For some it may come very quickly, almost instantly, as a gift of God to which they are called to be faithful.

For others it may take years. There is often a strong resistance, not wanting to belong or not wanting to believe that we are called to be with others, because to belong means also to die to some aspects of our being:

to our independence,
to our freedom to do things.

In each of us there is a struggle against belonging. We fear the call to claim and develop our gifts to become responsible for others.

We fear also the call to submit to the gifts of others. In each of us there is pride that prevents us from believing in the call and the promise of Jesus, and from giving ourselves in a love and humility that would enable us to receive from others.

Accepted or rejected

Each person with his or her history of being accepted or rejected, with his or her past history of inner pain and difficulties in relationships with parents, is different. But in each one there is a yearning for communion and belonging, but at the same time a fear of it.

Love is what we most want, yet it is what we fear the most. Love makes us vulnerable and open, but we can then also be hurt through rejection and separation. We can crave for love but then be frightened of losing our liberty and creativity.

We want to belong to a group but we fear a certain death in the group because we may not be seen as unique.

We want love but fear the dependence and commitment it implies; we fear being used, manipulated, smothered and spoiled.

In respect to love, communion and belonging we are all so ambivalent.

Growing in trust

The sense of belonging flows from trust: trust is the gradual acceptance of others as they are with their gifts and their limits, each one with the call of Jesus. And this leads to the realization that the body of community is not perfectly whole and cannot be, that this is our human condition. And it is all right for us to be less than perfect. We must not weep over our imperfections. We are not judged for being defective. Our God knows that in so many ways we are lame and half blind.

We will never win the olympics of humanity, racing for perfection, but we can walk together in hope, celebrating that we are loved in our brokenness:

> helping each other,
> growing in trust,
> living in thanksgiving,
> learning to forgive,
> opening up to others,
> welcoming them,

and striving to bring peace and hope to our world. So it is that we come to put down roots in community not because it is perfect and wonderful, but because we believe that Jesus has called us together. It is where we belong and are called to grow and to serve.

Shepherding

Love for the flock does not mean giving them ice cream on holidays. It means that we are prepared to sacrifice our reputation, to sacrifice ourselves. It means that we are committed to them and that we won't slide away under the cover of some law or pretext which is really a defence against commitment.

The flock quickly sense somebody who is deeply concerned for them, somebody who is open, ready to listen at any moment . . . The good shepherd will always be welcoming, always open, because he is concerned for his sheep and ready to lay down his life for them . . .

The sheep sense the difference between the shepherd who is really concerned for them and the hireling who slips away as soon as there is a problem. Children sense when their parents sacrifice a rise in position so that the father may be more present in the home. People sense when the shepherd is concerned for the whole flock, not just for one or two who are more 'interesting'. Some teachers can be more concerned with the two or three apparently more intelligent students: they fail to give enough attention to the little ones, the crippled, the hurt and the wounded, who in fact need their care even more than the others.

The good shepherd

Shepherds must be prepared to compromise themselves for their flocks, for they love their flocks. They are committed to each member, whatever their intelligence, or their beauty or age. They know each one by name and they sense the individual needs of each.

That is why it is important for the shepherd to be present to each member of the flock in a special way, saying something personal to each one. This is why they must know each by name, in so far as the name represents the deep person and his or her deep needs.

Good shepherds speak the language of the flock. Some shepherds do not, for they do not know all the ways the flock has of communicating. This does not mean that someone who is working with prisoners has to use spicier language than normal. Prisoners must sense that the shepherd really understands them, for it is only then that the shepherd will be able to nourish them.

Shepherds must be continually creative, for this is commitment towards people. When you love you create and re-create. When you are in deep communion with someone who is in need then you create ways of responding to his or her need.

Become a shepherd

Jesus does not come like a doctor, to heal us and then to leave us. This healer is a shepherd, the good shepherd who teaches us to walk in the paths of the Beatitudes. As the healer calls us to heal, so the shepherd calls us forth to be shepherds.

Each of us is a shepherd, in some way. A parent is a shepherd to a child, a teacher to a student, a priest to a parishioner; a friend can often be a shepherd to a friend, for they guide each other. All of us are called to shepherdhood in some way for we are all responsible one to another.

It is important to see how Jesus is a shepherd, to discover how we should be shepherds. One of the reasons that there is a good deal of confusion in this world is precisely because there are too few good shepherds, deeply committed to the flock, deeply committed to people. Shepherdhood is a commitment to people, whatever may happen ... if they are wounded I too am wounded.

It is important for us to delve a little into the meaning of shepherdhood, to understand the commitment that it implies, to discover the responsibility each one of us has, whatever our age, whatever our function.

Fragility and openness

The very struggle to build community is a gift of God and in accepting it we acknowledge it as a gift, not received once and for all, but one for which we must yearn and pray and labour day after day. Since community is a living, dynamic body, it is in continual movement. It evolves as people grow, as the whole body grows in welcoming new people, as other people leave and separate to create another body, just as the cells of the body separate and multiply. Each community, as well as each person, lives its pains of growth, its times of passage.

The danger for all of us is to want a community that is strong and competent with the security of wealth, good administration and structures, and experienced, competent, committed people. None of us like to live in insecurity, in fear of tomorrow. We are all like Peter, afraid of walking on the waters. So we can quickly close our hearts, forgetting the call of Jesus and how he brought us to life through his guiding hand.

Community and growth

Even the most beautiful community can never heal the wound of loneliness that we carry. It is only when we discover that this loneliness can become sacrament that we touch wisdom, for this sacrament is purification and presence of God.

If we stop fleeing from our own solitude, and if we accept our wound, we will discover that this is the way to meet Jesus Christ. It is when we stop fleeing into work and activity, noise and illusion, when we remain conscious of our wound, that we will meet God.

He is the Paraclete, the One who responds to our cry, which comes from the darkness of our loneliness . . .

Community life is there to help us not to flee from our deep wound, but to remain with the reality of love. It is there to help us believe that our illusions and egoism will be gradually healed if we become nourishment for others. We are in community for each other, so that all of us can grow and uncover our wound before the infinite, so that Jesus can manifest himself through it.

Littleness

Once we have discovered the mystery of covenant and the community as a body, many aspects of hierarchy, rivalry, competition and the need to prove ourselves to be the best begin to disappear. Difference is no longer seen as a threat but as a treasure.

True humanity is not based on hierarchy, with the best on top and the worst, the most ignorant on the bottom. There is no perfect model.

There is no ideal person. No one possesses all the gifts. To be the leader is not a sign that one is the best, the most popular; superiors are not superior.

Humankind is called to know itself as one body. And within the body of community, or the body of the family, each man and woman, old or young, must be respected, each one recognized for the value of their differences; each one is needed to fulfil a unique role. Then we can see the exercise of authority as just one gift among many, at the service of others . . . And at the heart, at the very centre of the body of community, there are the littlest, the weakest and the poorest, bringing the gift of the presence of Jesus as an icon, as a sacrament.

His merciful love

We must have long moments under the anaesthetic of quiet prayer, because Jesus can teach us certain things only if we are under an anaesthetic.

He can show us our poverty, our misery, the gravity of what we have done; only if at the same time he can show us the depths of his merciful love.

You can only discover your sin, if you discover at the same time the mercy of Jesus.

This is why, if you have to reprimand someone and say, 'You have done this, admit it'; if you only show the law and nonconformity to the law, you will find that no one can accept personal sin, no one. They will either find excuses or go away despairing. You must not reveal to people their sin, their poverty, without at the same time showing them that they are loved and that there is hope; that they can do better. If you show only the law, you crush; bringing despair and revolt. But if through all your attitudes you show how much you hope and believe in this person, then, and then only, can you show them what was not right.

Personal prayer

When everyday life is busy and difficult, it is absolutely essential for us to have moments alone to pray and meet God in silence and quietness. Otherwise, our activity motor will become overheated and whizz around like a chicken without a head.

The Little Sisters of Foucauld have a whole rhythm in their rule of prayer and solitude: an hour a day, a half day a week, a week a year and a year each ten years. Interdependence grows in community, but we have to avoid an unhealthy dependence. We have to take time alone with Our Father, with Jesus. Prayer is an attitude of trust in Our Father, seeking his will, seeking to be a presence of love for brothers and sisters. Each of us must know how to rest and unwind in silence and contemplation, heart to heart with God.

Do not be afraid that your momentary withdrawal will be detrimental and do not be afraid that an increase in your personal love for God will in any way diminish your love for your neighbour. On the contrary, it will enrich it.

Rhythm of prayer

We all have to find our own rhythm of prayer. For some of us, this will mean praying for hours at a time, for others, for fifteen minutes here and there. For all of us, it is being attentive to God's presence and will throughout the day.

Some of us need the stimulus of the word of God or saying the Our Father; others need to repeat the name of Jesus or Mary. Prayer is like a secret garden made up of silence and rest and inwardness. But there are a thousand and one doors into this garden and we all have to find our own.

If we do not pray, if we do not evaluate our activities and find rest in the secret part of our heart, it will be very hard to live. We will not be open to others, we will not be craftsmen of peace. We will live only from the stimuli of the present moment, and we will lose sight of our priorities and of the essential. We have to remember too that some purifications come only with the help of the Holy Spirit. Only God can shed light on some corners of our feelings and unconscious.

Communal prayer

Communal prayer is an important nourishment. A community which prays together, which enters into silence and adoration, is bound together by the action of the Holy Spirit. God listens in a special way to the cry which rises from a community. When we ask him, together, for a gift or grace, he listens and grants our request.

Jesus says that the Father will give whatever is asked in his name; all the more reason for him to give when it is a community that asks.

It seems to me that we do not yet have enough recourse to this communal prayer at l'Arche. Perhaps we are not yet simple or child-like enough. In spontaneous community prayer we sometimes feel a bit lost. It is sad, to me, that we do not use the very beautiful texts of the Church, that we do not know the Scriptures better. It is true that a text can lose its savour if it is used every day. But spontaneity can lose its savour too. We have to find a harmony between the texts that tradition gives us and the spontaneous prayer which springs from the heart.

With him and in him

To pray is essentially:

> to come to Jesus and to drink,
> to come to him as to a friend,
> to be in communion with him,
> to remain in his love,
> to trust him,
> and to follow him;
> it is to rest in him.

To pray is to cry out to Jesus and to the Paraclete, the One who answers the cry, when we cannot go on or when we fall and touch our pain and brokenness. It is to offer all this pain and the pain of the world, with him and in him to the Father. It is to let the Holy Spirit penetrate into our brokenness

> and lead us to wholeness
> and teach us how to love as he loves.

Prayer is to be in contact with our own centre; it is to be close to our own source; it is to let Jesus make his home in us and to make our home in him. It is to be guided by Jesus, our good shepherd.

Eucharist

The Eucharist is celebration, the epitome of the communal feast, because in it we relive the mystery of Jesus' gift of his own life for us. We relive in a sacramental way his sacrifice on the cross which opened up a new life for people, which liberated hearts from fear and for love and union with God, and for community. The Eucharist is the time of thanksgiving for the whole community. That is why the priest says, after the consecration: 'Grant that we, who are nourished by his body and blood, may be filled with his Holy Spirit and become one body, one spirit in Christ.' There we touch the heart of the mystery of community.

But the Eucharist is also an intimate moment when each of us is transformed through a personal meeting with Jesus. 'He who eats my flesh and drinks my blood abides in me, and I in him' (John 6:56). At the moment of consecration, the priest repeats Jesus' words: 'Take this, all of you, and eat it; this is my body which will be given up for you.' It is the 'given up for you' which is striking. It is only when we have eaten this body that we can give ourselves to others ... This sacrifice, which is also a wedding feast, calls us to offer our lives to the Father, to become bread for others, and to rejoice in the wedding feast of love.

The growth of light

We need to discover the nourishment of the Spirit and be determined to live by it . . . As we become conscious of the growth of light, of the death of aggressiveness and the birth of life, we must begin with our minds to see what this implies for our way of life. We must begin to see what will help the life of the Spirit to grow . . . It might be meeting together to pray, perhaps in humble charismatic prayer, filled with the joy of the Spirit, and openness to others – not condemning or judging, but flowing from the Spirit in quiet healing. It might be calling forth into quiet, silent contemplative prayer, where there are no words, but a deepening of peace, abiding at the feet of Jesus and learning to pray as Mary prayed: the quiet contemplation of Charles de Foucauld or Teresa of Avila, which is at the heart of the tradition of the saints through the ages.

It might be a prayer of peace, a prayer of repose, a prayer of great love which pulls us into long hours of just being possessed by the silence of God. It might be quiet recitation of the rosary, the peaceful naming of the word of God, the name of Jesus, the name of Mary, or just the quiet prayer of the liturgy, the reading of the psalms. There are all these forms of dialogue with our Father, with his Son and with the Spirit.

Do not be afraid

Insecurity and weakness are like a door through which passes the strength of God. Do not flee then from insecurity; do not seek to have all the answers. If you do, you risk turning away from God who is leading you in to the Kingdom.

'The Lord gives power to the weary and to the helpless ones he gives strength ... Those who trust in the Lord shall renew their strength. They shall soar up with wings, like eagles. They shall run and not be weary; they shall walk and never falter' (Isaiah 40:31).

If we are called to walk with the poor in community Jesus will always be there, saying: 'Do not be afraid, for I am with you' (John 6:20).

The guide

If we are to grow in love and to become more fully men and women of peace, we need a guide. All alone we shall quickly become discouraged, fall away, and seek the more trodden path. Without a guide it is difficult to recognize the fruits of the presence of God in our lives.

When we touch a point of pain, we will panic and run away. We need a wise and loving guide, a follower of Jesus . . . who will remind us of the call of Jesus and how he has been present in our lives, gently guiding us at all times; who will remind us that we are loved and called to walk with Jesus on the road of pain and compassion in resurrection.

Such a guide will not tell us what to do, but will listen and discern with us, our way in the Will of the Father. The guide will be able to put a name to what we are living. The guide will hold us in prayer, lovingly, calling the Spirit upon us, confirming us in our call, challenging us too and calling us to be true in all things . . .

The one who is guide can show us also the gift of the forgiveness of Jesus . . . who can carry all our sins and weaknesses, and to whom, as a gentle instrument of God's mercy, we can open our hearts . . .

Friendship

Each of us is called to fidelity, to commitment, even if this is simply the commitment of friend to friend. The friend senses the friend who is really committed. There are false friends who are there to laugh when we laugh, but not to weep when we weep. There are false friends who are there to profit from our intelligence or our possessions, but who disappear when we are sick or destitute or rejected.

A real friend, to whom we can say exactly what we feel, knowing that we will be listened to, encouraged and confirmed in love and tenderness, is an absolutely essential resource. When friendship encourages fidelity, it is the most beautiful thing of all. Aristotle calls it the flower of virtue, it has the gratuity of the flower. On the dark days, we need the refuge of friendship. When we feel flat or fed up, a letter from a friend can bring back peace and confidence. The Holy Spirit uses small things to comfort and strengthen us.

Rest in those we love

A friend sent me a text of Bernard of Clairvaux; I found it very beautiful:

'While I write this letter, you are present to me as I am sure I shall be present to you when you read it. We wear ourselves out scribbling to each other, but is the Spirit ever weary of loving? We find rest in those we love and we provide a resting place in ourselves for those who love us.'*

Letters can be a real nourishment.

We should not be afraid of loving people and telling them we love them. That is the greatest nourishment of all.

* Bernard of Clairvaux, letter 90.

Love one another

In every human being there is such a thirst for communion with another, a cry to be loved and understood – not judged or condemned; a yearning to be called forth as special and unique. But this communion with another implies exigencies: to come out of one's shell of protection; to become vulnerable in order to love and understand others, to call them forth as special and unique, to share and to give space and nourishment to them. That is where the pain and fear lie, even sometimes the impossibility to love.

Jesus calls his followers to love, to love one another as he loves them; not just to love others as one loves oneself. He proposes something new: to love one another with the very love of God; to see them with the eyes of the Lord. And we can only see and love them like Jesus if we ourselves have an experience in faith of Jesus loving us with a liberating love. It is only then that we can open ourselves up and become vulnerable and grow to greater openness to others and give our lives.

Man and woman in the vision of God

The difference between man and woman is a radical and fundamental one which permeates the depths of their consciousness and affects all human behaviour. It is at the beginnings of life itself. In Genesis 1:27 is said 'male and female he created them'. He wished that they be one, that they be 'one body' (Genesis 2:24).

Man and woman are complementary in their bodies and their psychology. They each discover their being in relation to God who created them; each in the image of God, they are called to become like God. Such is their fundamental ultimate goal in the universe.

However, they are also in the image of God in their union and their unity of love. Each one is with and for the other. Each one discovers his or her self in relationship to the other.

Union

When a man and a woman truly love each other, whether it be through the tenderness and communion of marriage or in celibacy and community life, there is nothing more beautiful. It is the gift of God to humanity. Their love is the root of the 'body' which is the community. It is the power of unity which will inspire all other unities; it is the power of healing which will inspire all other healings. It is fruitful with a spiritual fruitfulness . . .

Each one, alone, is fragile and incomplete, but through an authentic love which is communion and gift, a unity is given which draws us from our loneliness and makes us enter the heart of a God who is Father, Son, and Holy Spirit.

One body

To be one body is to be covenanted together,
each in need of the other,
each having a special gift to offer the other,
complementing the other.
They need each other to give life.

Alone man or woman can use wood to build a
    house;
alone each one can produce *things*.
But to create life,
man and woman must unite physically and in
    love.

Only God, the artist of life,
can make an object that is living,
with whom it is possible to enter into dialogue.
Yet through procreation, God gives to man and
    woman
the power to transmit life.
But in doing so they act, not as artists,
but as humble instruments of nature.
The child that will be born is of their flesh;
they will be able to enter into relationship with
    the child,
but they cannot create a child of their dreams.
They can only receive the child that is given to
    them.

Death

The death of someone we love is always shattering. To love is to carry another within oneself, to keep a special place in one's heart for him or her. This spiritual space is nourished by a physical presence; death, then, tears out a part of our own heart. Those who deny the suffering of death have never truly loved; they live in a spiritual illusion.

To celebrate death, then, is not to deny this laceration and the grief it involves, it is to give space to live it, to speak about it, and even to sing of it. It is to give mutual support, looking the reality in the face and placing all in the Heart of God in deep trust. Jesus did not come to abolish suffering and death, but he showed us the way to live them both fruitfully. We must penetrate the mystery of suffering by surrender and sacrifice.

Learning to forgive

As long as we refuse to accept that we are a mixture of light and darkness, of positive qualities and failings, of love and hate, of altruism and egocentricity, of maturity and immaturity, and that we are all children of the same Father, we will continue to divide the world into enemies – the 'baddies' and friends – the 'goodies'. We will go on throwing up barriers around ourselves, spreading prejudice.

When we accept that we have weaknesses and flaws, that we have sinned against God and against our brothers and sisters, but that we are forgiven and can grow towards interior freedom and truer love, then we can accept the weaknesses and flaws of others. They too are forgiven by God and are growing towards the freedom of love. We can look at all men and women with realism and love. We can begin to see in them the wound of pain that brings up fear, but also their gift which we can love and admire. We are all mortal and fragile, but we are all unique and precious. There is hope; we can all grow towards greater freedom. We are learning to forgive.

Forgiveness

Forgiveness is the source and the rock of those who share their lives:

> to forgive each day,
> to forgive and forgive and forgive,
> and to be forgiven just as many times . . .

Forgiveness is the cement that bonds us together: it is the source of unity; it is the quality of love; that draws togetherness out of separation. Forgiveness is understanding and holding the pain of another; it is compassion. Forgiveness is the acceptance of our own brokenness, yours and mine. Forgiveness is letting go of unrealistic expectations of others and of the desire that they be other than they are. Forgiveness is liberating others to be themselves, not making them feel guilty for what may have been. Forgiveness is to help people flower, bear fruit, and discover their own beauty . . .

Forgiveness is to follow Jesus, to be like him, for he came to give and to forgive, to take from the shoulders of people the yoke of guilt that locks them into a prison of sadness and sterility, and prevents them from flowing and living freely.

Love with a universal heart

We can only truly accept others as they are, and forgive them, when we discover that we are truly accepted by God as we are and forgiven by him. It is a deep experience knowing that we are loved and held by God in all our brokenness and littleness . . .

To accept responsibility for our sinfulness and hardness of heart, and to know that we are forgiven is a real liberation. I don't have to hide my guilt any more.

We can only really love our enemies and all that is broken in them if we begin to love all that is broken in our own beings.

We can only really love with a universal heart as we discover that we are loved by the universal heart of God.

Balance

It is difficult to make people understand that the ideal doesn't exist, that personal equilibrium and the harmony they dream of come only after years and years of struggle, and even then only as flashes of grace and peace. If we are always looking for our own equilibrium, I'd even say if we are looking too much for our own peace, we will never find it, because peace is the fruit of love and service to others. I'd like to tell the many people who are looking for this impossible ideal: 'Stop looking for peace, give yourselves where you are. Stop looking at yourselves -- look instead at your brothers and sisters in need. Be close to those God has given you today; and work with the references that are there . . . Then you will find peace. You will find rest and that famous balance you're looking for between the exterior and the interior, between prayer and activity, between time for yourself and time for others.'

But to be good instruments of God's love we must avoid being over-tired, burnt-out, stressed, aggressive, dispersed or closed up. We need to be rested, centred, peaceful, aware of the needs of our body, our heart and our spirit. Jesus says that there is no greater love than to give our lives. But let us not give over-tired, stressed and aggressive lives, but rather joyful ones!

Head, hands and heart

People consist of head, hands and heart. They are capable of knowledge, of skills and of the relationship of love. Activity and work, particularly interesting work – bring a certain fulfilment. But this is not sufficient. They need friends, someone in whom they can trust; someone with whom they can have a deep relationship and share their weakness and secrets.

Human beings need to be loved, need affection and tenderness. Without it, they harden. But some are afraid of love and relationships. They are afraid of becoming vulnerable and of being hurt in their hearts or of being rejected. They close themselves up and protect themselves . . .

The newborn child is totally weak. Without the protective love and tenderness of the mother and father the child will die. But if it is certain of love, it will be happy and at peace and will rest in the security of their love. The child will not fear its weakness and will not have to prove goodness, intelligence or power. The child just knows that it is loved; it believes and trusts. If its trust, however, is deceived, then the child will fall into the pits of sadness. If the child feels abandoned, it will die spiritually. Fortunately many children have that beautiful experience of knowing that they are unique and loved in a special way.

The gift of today

Jesus calls us forth to his patience and his impatience. He helps us gradually to accept people as they are, without judgement or condemnation, with all their defects, difficulties and bitterness, and their hopes, ambitions and capacities. He helps us to look at the other person and to understand, and when this understanding has been born, perhaps to help growth according to the music of his being, giving the nourishment necessary.

There are a lot of people who weep when it rains and then find the sun too hot when it comes out. In winter they long for summer, in summer for autumn . . . Small people pretend to be big, and old people dress themselves up to look young . . . instead of discovering the beauty of youth and of age as they come.

We should learn to rejoice in the gift that is today. Even if we fall sick, we should rejoice; for there's no point in fighting it and it's a good time for quiet reading and prayer. We should relax in sickness and relax in health, accepting both as gifts from the Spirit . . .

Disarmament

Our modern world has fantastic power and knowledge. Man has conquered the moon, delved into the secret of matter and discovered immense energies. We have amazing knowledge.

The only real knowledge necessary for the survival of the human race is lacking; the knowledge of how to transform violence and hatred into tenderness and forgiveness, how to stop the chain of aggression against the weak, how to see differences as a value rather than as a threat; how to stop people from envying those who have more, and incite them to share with those who have less.

The real question of today is disarmament, not only on the international scale but in terms of our own personal aggression. Is it possible for men and women to break down the barriers of prejudice and fear that separate groups and races and to create one people? Are we condemned to war or is peace possible?

Aggression

Often instead of dealing with our negative feelings directly we direct them towards others who are innocent.

There is the story of misplaced aggression. The director of a factory yells unjustly at a worker. The latter cannot respond directly so, when he gets home, his pent-up frustrations are unleashed against his wife who in turn yells at her daughter. The daughter then kicks the dog who chases the cat. And the story ends with the death of the mouse.

This seemingly funny story is alas the story of much that happens in groups and among people. We need to find someone weaker than ourselves upon whom we can put our negative feelings without endangering ourselves.

Differences among people very quickly become threatening. The white reject the black, the healthy reject the handicapped, the rich reject the poor, and vice versa. What is the source of all this hatred and division, prejudice and fear?

The road to transformation

When we begin to sense how far away we are from the Master of the Beatitudes, when we begin to sense how little we love our enemies, how aggressive we are, how little we are good shepherds, how little we really live in community, how little we strive to sense that we need to be healed and to be transformed, because God is calling us to something that we cannot possibly do by ourselves . . .

We cannot love an enemy; we flee from an enemy, we are aggressive towards him, we hurt and wound him. We disregard little people. We're frightened.

When we begin to sense all the security we have in our lives that prevents us opening ourselves to the Spirit, when we sense how comfortable we are, how we seek comfort rather than compassion and love -- then we are preparing the road to transformation . . .

I am poor

When I discover
  that I am poor,
     that I am confused,

but, that you call me
  by my name,
     that you love me,

then,
  this is the
     moment of transformation:
       man and woman transformed
        into
         Jesus,

       living Jesus,
        born of the Spirit,
         which all Christians should be.

This will come only when that miracle takes place
and I discover that I am loved as I am, in my own
poverty, and that Jesus will use me in spite of my
stupidity, my lowliness, my weakness.

Abide in my love

Jesus often uses the word 'abide'. To abide in Jesus is what prayer is about. We must live this word and open up the chalice of our being to the presence of God, enter into his silence.

We must learn to rest in that peace which comes when he touches our hearts. We must know that this peace is the presence of God, that this is how God speaks to us – through this love which touches us at our core and flows through all our being and plunges us into silence. We must be open to this peace.

The healing and transforming process is begun and completed in this abiding in Jesus in prayer. It is to the extent that we abide in him that we are gradually transformed, and discover that our enemies cease to be enemies, and that we can love them. It is to the extent that we abide in Jesus that we can become a peacemaker and thus a child of God.

> Happy the peacemakers;
> they shall be called sons of God. (Matthew 5:9)

Where your treasure is

Your treasure is there, where your heart lies . . .
Where is your treasure? Is it in Jesus? If not, it is
not too late; it is never too late to sell much, to
sell all, in fact, to find him and to follow him.
You remember what Jesus said of the pearl: 'A
pearl of great price was hidden in a field and
somebody who collected pearls knew this. So, he
sold everything and bought the field' (cf. Matthew
13:46).

It is not too late for us to find the treasure and
we must find it because we are called to help
many. We must be able to point out where this
treasure lies. For all must find him, Jesus poor,
Jesus merciful, Jesus meek, Jesus now and again
violent, Jesus sometimes passionate and Jesus
humble, Jesus tender, Jesus loving, Jesus just,
Jesus hungry and thirsty for justice.

Peacemaking

Peacemaking does not begin in big meetings or street marches, but in welcoming with compassion others with whom we live and share work, those who threaten us because they are different; those who hurt us, 'our enemies', because they tread on our toes, do not give us enough consideration or the place we feel should be ours.

Peacemaking begins at home as we carry the wounds of others, and allow them to carry ours, in compassion, uplifting them, and nourishing their gifts.

In this way, a family or a community is built up, not founded on laws, administration or good organization – necessary and important as these may be – but gently developed through loving relationships.

The first peacemakers are the broken people themselves: it is their cry of pain, their cry for love, the primal cry springing from their brokenness which attracts and calls forth people, but disturbs them too: it both heals and hurts. Jesus said:

> 'When I am lifted up, then I will draw all to me.' (John 12:32)

Opening up our being

Let us open ourselves to the healing, forgiving Spirit of Jesus. Let us open up all the pains of the past, the wounds that came from the moment of our conception – wanted or unwanted – and from the months we were carried in our mother's womb; the wounds from our early childhood when we felt rejected or stifled, unloved in our being and unrecognized in our gifts; the wounds coming from all the failures of the past; our incapacity to love and give life, the people we have hurt because of our sinfulness, pride or fears, and the barriers we have built around our vulnerability.

Let us allow the healing, forgiving Spirit of Jesus to penetrate our whole being, and lead us to wholeness. Then will rise from that very darkness a new understanding of others.

Mary

In order to welcome the gift of the body of Jesus
  we must look more fully at the woman
  who conceived him
  and gave him birth –
  Mary.

For none like her
  enveloped his body,
  touched his body,
  loved his body,
  washed his body,
  venerated his body.

The body of Christ
  flowed from her body,
  the fruit of her womb.
  It was her body that nourished his body;
  her breasts gave
  him the energy and nourishment to grow;
  her touch protected him
  and revealed to him that he was loved;
  her presence made him sing with joy;
  the light in her eyes called forth the light in his.

Before she was touched and sanctified by his
words, she had been touched and sanctified by his
body,
  the Temple of God,
  the sacred place where God resides.

I thirst

And Jesus cries out:
'I thirst.'
'I need water!'
'I need love.'

'My God, my God, why have you abandoned me?'

His broken body hangs on the wood
    limp
    dirty
    covered with blood
    ugly with wounds;
    his face lined with agony,
    no beauty,
    no comeliness:
    a man of sorrows.

And during all the time he hung there the woman
    was beside him.

Mary was there,
standing at the foot of the cross,
a sign of hope, of trust, of love.
She stood firm,
this silent woman of compassion,
not crushed,
not fleeing from the pain.

The eyes of the poor

Sometimes the greatest resource of all can be a small gesture of kindness from someone who is poor. It is often a gentle look from someone who is vulnerable which relaxes us, touches our heart and reminds us of what is essential.

One day I went with some sisters of Mother Teresa to a slum in Bangalore where they looked after some people with leprosy ... The people there had light in their eyes. All I could do was hold the instruments the sisters were using, but I was glad to be there. The expressions and smiles of the people seemed to reach right into me and renew me. When I left, I felt an inexplicable joy.

The smile

My heart is transformed by the smile of trust given
by some people who are terribly fragile and weak.
They call forth new energies from me. They seem
to break down barriers and so to bring me a new
freedom.

It is the same with the smile of a child: even the
hardest heart can't resist. Contact with people
who are weak and are crying out for communion,
is one of the most important nourishments in our
lives. When we let ourselves be really touched by
the gift of their presence, they leave something
precious in our hearts.

Our struggle for peace

At l'Arche we are not alone in our struggle for peace and our desire to live with broken people. We are not the only followers of Jesus who walk the downward path, into the pains of the earth, in the hope of rebirth and growth towards freedom. All over the earth little communities in flower, followers of Jesus radiating light in so many places of pain:

> little lights shine in refugee camps
> in Cambodia, eyes of love and compassion
> burn in the horror of our prisons, faces
> of hope glow in the ghettos, brothers
> and sisters, missionaries of charity,
> close to those who are dying, bathing
> them with love; little sisters and
> brothers of Jesus, close to the poor,
> discovering the beauty in them.

And in every parish too, in every home, in every heart that welcomes a wounded person there is the quiet presence of Jesus, consoling, loving, announcing the good news. Yes, all over the world the poor are discovering their value and their beauty: the light of the world is present in their bodies and their inmost being, God is revealed.

The great secret of Jesus

The poor and the weak have revealed to me the great secret of Jesus. If you wish to follow him you must not try to climb the ladder of success and power, becoming more and more important. Instead, you must walk *down* the ladder, to meet and walk with people who are broken and in pain. The light is there, shining in the darkness, in the darkness of their poverty. The poor with whom you are called to share your life are perhaps the sick and the old; people out of work, young people caught up in the world of drugs, people angry because they were terribly hurt when they were young, people with disabilities or sick with AIDS, or just out of prison; people in slums or ghettos, people in far-off lands where there is much hunger and suffering, people who are oppressed because of the colour of their skin, people who are lonely in overcrowded cities, people in pain.

We are discovering too that the life-giving Jesus is hidden in them. He is truly there. If you become a friend of the poor, you become a friend of Jesus.

If you enter into a close relationship with those who are poor, you enter into an intimate relationship with Jesus and you will be led into the heart of the Beatitudes.

Cells of the one body

Today as yesterday Jesus is calling us to follow him, to walk in his footsteps.

He is calling you and me to be like him, wherever and whoever we are, whatever we think of ourselves.

To live as he lived,
to love as he loved,
to speak as he spoke,
to offer our lives as he offered his,
to do what he did,
to do even greater things
because of his going to the Father.

By ourselves this is impossible. How can we live and love as he did, except through the mysterious gift and power which he gives us through his Spirit, so that we become his face, his hands, his heart and body?

Not just you and I alone, as individuals, but together in the body of community. And again not a group, separated and isolated, thinking it is the best and sufficient unto itself, but linked to others, to other communities, all cells of the one body, the Church, united with men and women all over the world.

Giving life

When Jesus meets the woman of Samaria, he does not begin by speaking to her from the top of a pedestal, but from the pit of his own needs – his cry of thirst:

'Give me to drink.'

She belonged to what we call 'the fourth world':

she had lived with five men
and the man she was then living with
was not her husband.

She was utterly broken:

her self-image shattered,
ridden with guilt,
rejected by her own people
who were themselves rejected.

Jesus looks at this woman, who others scoff at and despise, the 'dirty prostitute', and he says

'You can do something for me,
I need your help.'

The ways of God are to bring down the powerful from their thrones and to lift up the lowly; not to judge or condemn but to meet people where they are and to give life.

The Church

The Church is the assembly of believers, those who have been called out of a world full of sin and hate and fear, but also remain in it as a witness of love and a sign of the resurrection. The Church is those who trust in Jesus, who recognize in him the Lamb of God who saves and heals, and frees us from guilt. But it is also a Church of pain, because it is a Church of sinners who believe and do not believe, who trust and do not trust, who walk in light but also in darkness. The secret face of the Bride, the Body, is full of light. But the visible face of the Church is clouded. Yet we should not be disturbed by the clouds; there is sun shining behind them.

The wisdom of the little ones

I am convinced that Jesus gives himself to the hearts of the littlest and the poorest. He has great joy in living in their hearts. The poor show us the path. It is a privilege for us in l'Arche to be with them and to be witnesses of the truth of the words of Jesus: 'Blessed are you Father, Lord of heaven and earth, for having hidden these things from the wise and the learned and revealed them to the littlest ones' (Matthew 11:25) . . .

The person with a mental handicap, even as an adult, maintains some of the characteristics of a child, being spontaneous, simple, and often trusting. It is because of that they are closer to the God of Love, less a prisoner of pride, riches and power. Living more at the level of the heart, they are spontaneously attracted to the person of Jesus, who manifests himself in tenderness, goodness, compassion and forgiveness.

So many things in us desire greatness and power (even religious power) . . . We are seduced by the riches and pleasures of the world. The person with a mental handicap reveals to me all the hardness of my heart, all my wounds, my pride, my fear of communion and of love. The really simple faith of the person with a mental handicap calls me also to simplify my faith and to become a child.

Jesus and the poor

Jesus came to our earth to live with poor men and women, and he asks us his disciples to follow his example, to seek out the poor, to allow ourselves to be formed by them, to give them our heart. We then receive a precious gift: the love of the poor man's heart, a reflection of the heart of the poor man Jesus; and we are fulfilled.

In becoming presence, in living a relationship with the poor, we discover the contemplative dimension of love: how Jesus is hidden in the heart of the weak; how the face of the poor is the reflection of the face of Jesus.

Let us hope and pray that many places, many oases will appear in the Church where the poorest among us can be welcomed and through gestures of tenderness they can discover the tenderness of the Father for them, and that through the heart of Jesus' disciples, they may discover the very heart of God.

The elder brother of us all

Since the day the word became flesh
and became one among us,
each human being is intimately
linked to Jesus.
The word became man in every way except sin:
a human, vulnerable heart

with the capacity to love
and the capacity to weep and suffer pain
and so be able to forgive and be compassionate.

Jesus is one of us, he is one of our flesh.
He is the elder brother of us all,
brother of the littlest and weakest person
who may not even know him by name.

He is the lover of each man and woman,
for each one is the work of his hands,
each one is the image of God,
each one has the light of God burning within;
he cares for each one; . . .
And he says so clearly that
he is the hungry and the thirsty,
he is the person in prison or sick in hospital,
he is the stranger, the person lying naked
in the street.
Here lies the mystery.
The body of Christ is humanity.

Celebrating together

Celebration expresses the true meaning of community in a concrete and tangible way. So it is an essential element in community life. Celebration sweeps away the irritations of daily life; we forget our little quarrels. The aspect of ecstasy in a celebration unites our hearts; a current of life goes through us all. Celebration is a moment of wonder when the joy of the body and the senses are linked to the joy of the spirit. It unites everything that is most human and most divine in community life.

The liturgy of the celebration – which brings together music, dance, song, light, and the fruit and flowers of the earth – brings us into communion with God and each other, through prayer, thanksgiving and good food. (And the celebratory meal is important!)

The harder and more irksome our daily life, the more our hearts need these moments of celebration and wonder. We need times when we all come together to give thanks, sing, dance, and enjoy special meals. Each community, like each people, needs its festival liturgy.

Time to relax

Celebrations certainly have a role in helping people to accept the sufferings of everyday life by offering them the chance to relax and let go. But to see them as nothing but a form of escapism or drug, is to fail to understand human nature. We all . . . live a daily life which brings its own weariness; we make things dirty, we clean them, we plough, sow, and harvest.

As we need the day for work, activity, prayer, rejoicing and the night for sleep; as we need the four seasons with their different climates; so too we need the drudgery of dailiness and the joys of celebration; we need the work day and the sabbath. Our human hearts need something beyond the limitations and frustrations of the daily grind. We thirst for a happiness which seems unattainable on earth. We crave the infinite, the universal, the eternal – something which gives a sense to human life and its irksome daily routines. A festival is a sign of heaven. It symbolizes our deepest aspiration – an experience of total communion.

Love of self

It seems strange to affirm that we have to be disciplined in rest, relaxation and nourishment. So often discipline is equated to work and relaxation to 'no discipline'. If we do not choose the nourishment we need or do not get sufficient sleep, we are lacking in discipline.

It is never easy to find the harmony between rest, relaxation and nourishment on one hand, and generosity and availability on the other. Only the Holy Spirit can teach us to love ourselves sufficiently in order to give our lives as totally as possible. If we are not well, in good shape, joyful and nourished, we will not give life to others but will communicate sadness and emptiness.

When we are young we need to *do* lots of things – even for Jesus and the Kingdom. There is so much life and energy in us. And, of course, there is the risk of over-doing and of becoming *too* responsible, of wanting to be the saviours of the world! This has always been a danger for me. In 1976, my body reacted and I fell sick and was in the hospital for two months. This sickness was a turning point in my life. It brought me back to the earth of my body; it taught me to slow down, to listen rather than to speak or do; to relax in communion rather than to accomplish.

Path to unity

The broken Body of the Church is the source of so many tears. Maybe today Christians are not fully one in their beliefs, their organization and their structures. But they can be one in their love and in their yearning to follow Jesus, not always knowing the path ahead, which will be revealed little by little by the Spirit.

They can be one as together they walk down the ladder with Jesus, meeting Jesus in the poorest and weakest.

It is true that Christians of different traditions cannot drink today from the same chalice of the blood of Christ but we can all drink together from the same chalice of suffering: the sufferings of division, of brokenness in our world. Together we can pour the sweet oil of compassion upon the wounds of humanity. Unity will come not only around the treasure of the body of Jesus,

> his broken, rising body
> hidden in the Eucharist,

but also through the treasure of the broken body of Jesus in the poor.

Is not this the most direct path to unity?

Beatitude

Blessed are you in your poverty; you are not shut in in the false world of convention, riches, and human security.

Blessed are you because you are gentle; you refuse violence and aggressiveness; you allow yourself to be led by the Spirit into the world of tenderness and patience.

Blessed are you because you hunger and thirst for justice; your heart beats in the rhythm of the heart of Jesus.

Blessed are you because your heart is pure; you do not accept compromises.

Blessed are you because you are merciful; you attach your heart to misery; you will receive mercy and no one will see your sin.

Blessed are you because at all times and at every moment you want to be an instrument of peace; seeking unity, understanding, and reconciliation above all things.

Blessed are you because you have allowed your conscience to develop; you have not been swayed by what people might say about you and you have acted as a free individual; you have accepted persecution; you have not been afraid to proclaim the truth.

Sources and index

Source references (in order of appearance) are abbreviated thus:

TCM   Tape of Address to the Community at Minster Abbey
BB   *The Broken Body* (DLT, 1988)
BNA   *Be Not Afraid* (Griffin House, 1975)
CG   *Community and Growth* (revised edn, DLT, 1989)
F of J   *Followers of Jesus* (Alive Press, 1973)
MW   *Man and Woman He Made Them* (DLT, 1985)
C of l'A *The Challenge of l'Arche* (DLT, 1982)
EL l'A   Edited Letters of l'Arche, no. 56, p. 2 (June 1988)
Tro   Trosly publication, 'To Welcome the Poor is to Welcome Jesus' (trans. of article in *Vie Consacrée*, Brussels, March 1981)

The figures in bold type in the index refer to the pages of Readings in this book. They are followed by the Sources.